More Quilts and Coverlets

from
The American Museum in Britain

by Shiela Betterton

The American Museum in Britain

Published by the American Museum in
Britain, Bath, England.

© SHIELA BETTERTON

ISBN 0 9504971 7 7

Printed in Great Britain by
Butler & Tanner Ltd, Frome and London

Foreword

'Quilts and Coverlets' by Shiela Betterton, published by the American
Museum in 1978 and reprinted in 1982, has sold over nine thousand
copies. That it has proved to be such a success shows how the interest
in the subject of quilts has grown since the collection in the Museum
was started over thirty years ago. Those who already have a copy on
their shelves will find that 'More Quilts and Coverlets' not only contains
fresh illustrations but that the subject is approached differently; both
books contain the essential information as to the history and origin of
quilts but both have been intended to stand on their own.

In 1957, Dr Dallas Pratt, co-founder with John Judkyn of the
American Museum in Britain, visited the Shelburne Museum in
Vermont and saw the quilt collection there. It was one of the few that
had been formed up to that time. Much impressed he and John Judkyn
obtained permission to include some of the Shelburne quilts in the
exhibition of British examples of the craft which Mr Judkyn staged in
May 1958 at Freshford Manor. That was, in all probability, the first
time that American quilts were exhibited in Britain, and it marked the
beginning of the collection in the American Museum, which is not only
the best outside the United States of America, but ranks high among
collections there. From those enthusiastic beginnings the collection in
the museum has grown to consist of over 160 quilts and some 36 woven
coverlets as well as 40 hooked rugs and 30 Navajo weavings.

For fifteen years, during this period of growth, Shiela Betterton has
been Curator of Textiles in the Museum. What many consider to be
the dull, dry world of a museum is informed by human interest and
devotion. Conversely, it is the collections, the objects themselves, which
inspire interest and scholarship. The collection of quilts in the American
Museum has been a source of constant interest to Shiela Betterton. She
has studied the subject and lectured on it in many places. Yet, without
the collection, without the support and interest which the American
Museum has given her, the pleasure and instruction which she has been
able to give to others would not have been possible. It is this inter-
relationship between the public and the curator, as with the curator and
the collections, which can all too easily be overlooked or unappreciated.
Without Shiela Betterton's personal interest in the subject, without her
conscientiousness and her willingness to share and extend her
knowledge, both the American Museum and its visitors would be the
poorer.

Ian Lowe

Director

Acknowledgement

Grateful acknowledgement is made to the Esmée Fairbairn Charitable Trust for the generous grant towards the cost of publication.

Contents

Introduction

To many people the words patchwork and quilting are synonymous, but they are two entirely different forms of needlework. Patchwork is the sewing together of small pieces of fabric, usually geometric in shape, to make the top of a bedcover. To this is attached a backing with a padding in between, and the three layers are held together by quilting, a pattern in running stitch which is the last process in the making of the quilt. Some quilt tops may be of plain fabric and some may have appliqué patterns instead of patchwork.

It is often assumed, when considering old American quilts that they were made of patchwork, but although it can be ascertained from contemporary literature that quilting skills were taken to America by early colonists, there is no mention of patchwork. The Puritans considered needlework a virtuous occupation and women emigrating from Europe took with them their textile skills, including a knowledge of plain sewing.

Needlework was an important economic factor in the life of a woman in colonial days. It was essential for her to know how to prepare yarn and to make and repair clothing and other household textiles, and because of the limitations of early looms she also had to know how to make decorative effects with her needle. Quilting was part of this work. When warm and comfortable beds were a necessity and on the housewife's shoulders rested the responsibility for ensuring that they were provided, the making of bed furnishings was one of her main concerns. Most of the fabric was hand spun and hand woven from the mattress covers through the various layers – cases for feather beds and pillows, bedcurtains, valences, blankets and coverlets, and of course the top quilt which would be the most beautiful of all. In the days when the best bed was often in the parlour, exquisite stitchery and bed hangings were one way of demonstrating the housewife's needlework skills.

When America was a colony the mother country did little to encourage textile manufacture and despite the very early establishment of a textile factory at Rowley, Massachusetts, weaving remained largely a cottage industry until after the War of Independence. Deprived of facilities to manufacture their own textiles, the American colonists had to import from Europe and the east by way of Britain. Fabrics such as ginghams, dimity and damask, together with Indian chintzes and calicoes imported by the British East India Company, began to be available in America.

Many of the early textiles were blue dyed, possibly because indigo is a reliable dye, fast and strong enough to cover small discolourations and imperfections in the cloth. Until about 1750 textiles were printed in black, reds, purples and browns, all derived from madder. However, the Turkey Red dye, long known in the east and the first permanent red dye, was introduced into America about 1829 and from then on there was a proliferation of red and white quilts, often with green added.

The technique of quilting has been known for hundreds of years, coming to Europe from the east. In mediaeval times quilted jackets were worn under metal armour to prevent chafing and light troops had only a quilted jacket for protection. Bedcovers were quilted for warmth and in the eighteenth century both men and women wore quilted clothing.

It was a tradition that an American girl should have up to twelve quilts in her 'hope chest', possibly thirteen, the thirteenth being her bride's quilt. She began to piece the 'tops' at a very early age, but as a general rule they were not backed and quilted until she became engaged.

Leisure meant time for sewing and lack of contact with neighbours meant that women had to rely on pursuits that could be carried out in the home. The majority of quilts would be made and finished at home by the mother and her daughters. Others were quilted at a quilting bee, which was a welcome social occasion, particularly in the lives of pioneer women who lived far apart. Many quilting bees lasted a whole day. The largest room in the house was cleared and one or more quilting frames might be set up; if there was not room in the house the frames might be put up in a barn. The women would bring lunch with them and those who were not quilting took turns in the kitchen. Good needlewomen were always sought after and those whose sewing was not quite up to standard threaded needles and helped generally. When their work for the day was done the men joined the party; the quilt frames were put away and the hostess provided as grand a supper as she was able. After the meal there were usually games, music and dancing and the whole family took part.

Many women kept diaries or journals in which they recorded everyday happenings. Sometimes there is mention of patchwork, but more often the note reads 'Put quilt in frame' or 'Quilt finished, took out of frame', and one woman wrote with feeling, 'Oh, what a constant round of sweeping and dusting, so many cares, tried to finish the quilt'. It is from these same journals that we learn of work made by children, who often were set to learn the alphabet whilst they were sewing patchwork.

Making patchwork became so much part of a woman's life that by the middle of the nineteenth century designing patchwork quilt patterns had become one of the major forms of domestic folk art.

The Museum's collection illustrates many of these patterns.

Whole Cloth Quilts

Before the American War of Independence best quilts were very similar to those made in the British Isles. Many of these were solid colour, whole cloth, with no patchwork or applique, just a lovely quilted pattern tying the layers of cloth together.[1]

After 1630 many colonists brought sheep to America and the growing of flax and the manufacture of linen were encouraged, so quilt tops might be made from wool or linen or a mixture of the two linsey wolscy. Calamanco, a fine worsted which was often glazed (by heat and pressure), was imported from England together with the sheep's wool for the padding. The domestic wool clip was barely sufficient for home needs. The calamanco was also used for making quilted petticoats and the quilting patterns on both quilts and petticoats are very similar. As looms were narrow the top of the quilt was often made of several pieces of fabric joined together. The backing was homespun linen or wool.

Chintzes from England, Europe and India were imported into America and proved extremely popular for both dress and furnishings. Although American cotton became a staple crop in the 1760s it was not until about 1800 that cotton yarn could be made strong enough for weaving, and so the American cotton printing industry did not get under way until the early nineteenth century.

Some of the earliest fabric printing was done by wood blocks, but after 1750 printing from copper plates was possible. It was a long and expensive process to engrave the design on the plate, but it made possible the printing of designs with much larger repeats than had been possible with wood blocks and much finer detail could be obtained. Roller printing started in the first quarter of the nineteenth century, but for some years all three forms of printing were carried on at the same time.

Most whole cloth quilts made of printed fabric date from 1785 when increased amounts of printed textiles were available to the American market, and 1845 when the quality of the printing had greatly declined.

[1] Shiela Betterton. Quilts and Coverlets. The American Museum in Britain, 1978 and 1982, pp 11–15.

Game Birds
Quilt
L. 84 in   213 cm
W. 68 in   173 cm
Gift of Dr Dallas Pratt

A quilt which is very difficult to date. The top, made from four panels (two of 23 inches, two of 11 inches joined together) is one of a series of 'Game Birds' prints which were popular about 1810. The padding is thick cotton and the quilt has been 'tied' not quilted. The binding round the edge is a late nineteenth century cotton but the backing is of tan homespun. This could be an early quilt rebound, or the fabric carefully hoarded.

c 1810

Quilt
L. 98 in   249 cm
W. 100 in   254 cm
Gift of Mr and Mrs Reginald P.
Rose

Four breadths of fabric make the top of the quilt. The blue ground with red and white corinthian columns is now slightly faded. The backing is cotton with a very fine blue and white stripe and the binding a striped homespun. The quilting in the border is a pattern of trailing leaves and in the centre an all over pattern of double diamonds. The quilting bears no relation to the top.

Early nineteenth century

Wood Block Quilt
L. 84 in   213 cm
W. 72 in   183 cm

The pattern of pineapples, birds, stars, fruit and foliage has been applied by wood block printing to coarse home spun linen. The artist was not a professional but probably a talented amateur. The backing is homespun linen and the quilting is a chevron pattern covering the whole top of the quilt.

New York
c 1800

Quilt
L.   99 in   251 cm
W. 120 in   305 cm
Gift of Mrs Helen S. Clark

Five pieces of printed cotton dress fabric have been joined to make the top. The colouring is now almost all blue, the pink having nearly faded out. The quilt is lightly padded and has a fine homespun linen backing. The quilting is diagonal all over. Two corners have been cut to accommodate the posts of a four poster bed.

This coverlet belonged to Lucretia Hasseltine Kendall Clark (nee Kimball) who was born in 1853, a direct descendant of Dr John Robinson, Minister of the Pilgrim Fathers at Leyden. She was educated partly in Heidelberg where she met her future husband James Edmund Clark, a Quaker, whom she married in Boston in 1879. She led an active life as a teacher, in many fields of Quaker activity and in bringing up her family. Although all her married life was spent in England and in old age she retired to live in the midst of her husband's family in Somerset, she remained an American at heart.

c 1879

Pieced Quilts

The reasons for making patchwork originally would have been repair
and economy. Many countries have a tradition of patchwork of some
sort, but the mosaic patchwork which we know today did not develop
until the eighteenth century when fabric became more easily obtainable.

Early patterns were almost always geometric making the best possible
use of materials available, and straight lines were easy to sew with the
simplest of all stitches, running stitch. All women kept a scrap bag, a
jumble of old and new fabrics which could be utilised when needed to
make the tops of the family bedcovers.

The block technique, the making of one square of a given design at
one time evolved gradually and was a form of working which fitted in
with the conditions under which it was used and developed. The
geometric pieces making up the blocks made the most economical use
of cloth, and in small overcrowded houses making separate blocks
lessened storage problems. It was not until all the blocks were joined
together that space was needed. From this method of working there
developed a host of patterns, as once several blocks had been made
there were countless ways in which they could be put together to
produce different patterns.

The continuing westward expansion lasting into the twentieth century
meant that there was always a need for warm bedding, and women
trekking westwards continued to meet the challenge of finding new ways
of piecing together their scraps of cloth. Once the block method of
working had been established the skilful blending of shapes and colours
enhanced simple patterns; it needed an artistic eye to visualise the whole
quilt top when making just one block.

British influence is obvious from the use of the medallion format in
the eighteenth century and early nineteenth century. Often the central
motif was pieced and the many borders could be pieced or solid fabric.
Early in the nineteenth century cotton manufacturers began to print
panels specially to be used as the central motif of a quilt top. These
were often floral but others commemorated some historical event.

As early as 1830 patterns for quilt blocks were being published
regularly in American women's magazines and by the end of the century
many were being syndicated in newspapers and magazines throughout
the country.

The designs for American embroidery, and through embroidery for
quilting patterns stemmed from a number of different sources.
Immigrants from all over the world brought with them design traditions
from their homelands, and from time to time these patterns would be
injected with a new lease of life by succeeding waves of immigrants. At
an early date there were dame schools and schools for embroidery and
teachers encouraged the drawing of patterns and they also imported
books from which patterns could be taken. Another design source was
the New World itself and the women were not slow to give appropriate
names to their patterns. Names were taken from everyday objects –

'Dresden Plate', 'Churn Dash'; the environment – 'Windmill', 'Corn and Beans', 'Rocky Road to Kansas'; the Bible – 'Job's Tears', 'Crown of Thorns'; flowers – the many rose and tulip patterns; trees – 'Pine Trees', 'Oak Leaves'; Animals – 'Bear's Paw', 'Turkey Tracks'. After the Civil War the 'Log Cabin' pattern became very popular. It is a very adaptable pattern as the proportions can vary and the blocks can be joined together to form many different designs. The 'Princess Feather' pattern seems to date from the 1850s.

Many motifs were symbolic. Pineapples denoted hospitality, pomegranates fruitfulness, oak leaves long life and it was considered unlucky to have hearts on anything but a Bride's quilt.

The quilting pattern on a pieced quilt often just outlines the geometric shapes or perhaps there is one pattern which covers the whole quilt irrespective of the piecing. However, where white blocks alternate with pieced blocks, there is usually very intricate quilting on them.

Calamanco Quilt
L. 112 in   285 cm
W. 99   250 cm
Gift of Mrs Reginald Rose

The centre rectangle has been pieced from moreen, and other eighteenth century furnishing fabrics. The pink moreen has been 'watered'. The border of deep indigo blue calamanco has been heavily glazed and two corners have been cut out to accommodate the bedposts. The backing of an inferior homespun indigo woollen cloth and the padding is dark brown sheep's wool. There is diagonal quilting over the piecing and magnificent feather quilting in the border.

Late eighteenth or early nineteenth century

Nine-Patch Chain Quilt

Square 102 in 259 cm

This quilt, known as the 'Bridal Chest Quilt' was made by a bride of English descent living in Chester Co., Pennsylvania from 3,556 pieces of over one hundred different early prints. Each square in the nine-patch pattern is just one inch. The nine-patch blocks and associated triangles flow diagonally across the quilt. The border is an English copper plate chintz and the backing tan glazed cotton. The quilting in a large wine-glass pattern covers the whole quilt with complete disregard for the piecing.

c 1832

Silk Patchwork
Square 55 in   133 cm
Gift of Mrs Paul Moore

The subtle colours of this piece of patchwork are set off by the black satin border. Each $3\frac{1}{2}$ inch square has a $2\frac{1}{2}$ inch square set on point inside it. The setting strips are black satin also. There is no padding and the backing is gold silk.

c 1880

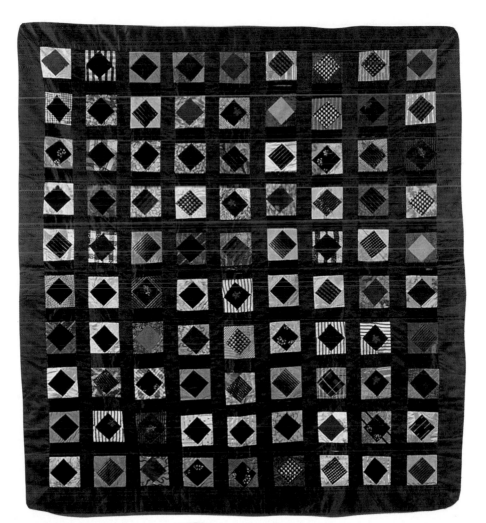

**Double Irish Chain
Quilt**
Square 75 in   191 cm
Gift of Mrs Elizabeth Frost

Typical Double Irish Chain pattern pieced from red and white cotton.
Feather roses have been quilted in the white blocks with diagonal
quilting over the pieced blocks. Made by Mary Elizabeth Plowman
Kschinka (grandmother of the donor) in Fort Leavenworth, Kansas.

Late nineteenth century

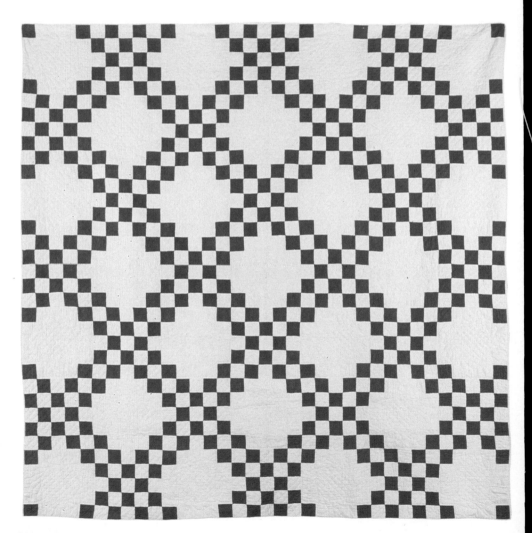

Irish Chain
Quilt
L. 84 in 215 cm
W. 73 in 186 cm
Gift of Mrs Joan Lynes

The coloured squares making up the pattern are just three quarters of an inch and are made into a 9-patch block. These are all set with white to make a variation on the Irish Chain pattern. The wide border is pale pink and quilted with a cable pattern, and the backing is of the same pink. Hearts have been quilted in the white blocks.

Kentucky
1930s

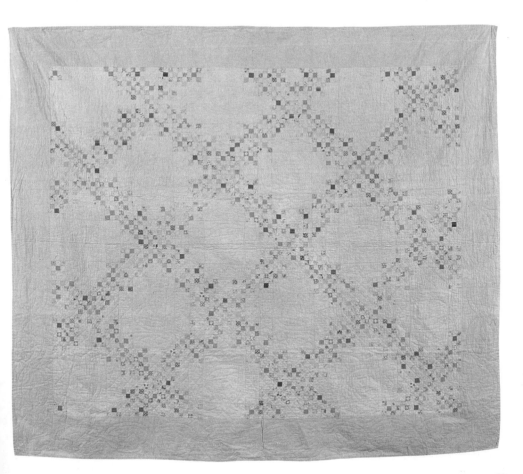

**Grandmother's Flower
Garden
Quilt**
L. 79 in   200 cm
W. 75 in   190 cm
*Gift of Mrs Eleanor Ball Hewitt-
Myring*

The hexagonal motifs have been pieced of printed cottons, mainly
reddish browns and blues with acid green sprigged cotton between
the motifs. This same cotton has been used for the border and the
backing. The quilting is outline. Made by Sarah Cannon Watts Ball
at Watts Plantation, near Laurens, South Carolina, (great
grandmother of the donor).

Pre 1860

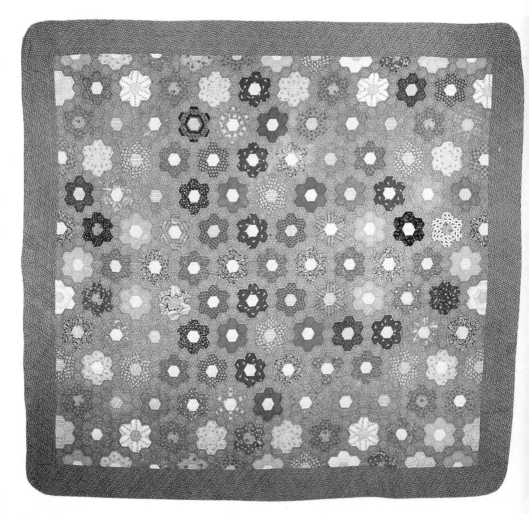

Quilt Top
L. 63 in   160 cm
W. 69 in   175 cm

Hexagonal shapes cut from tie silks have been pieced to make further hexagons, linked by small black silk diamonds. The border which has been added later is of navy blue silk patterned with white. This piece of work has never been backed or quilted and all piecing was done by hand over papers.

c 1880/1890

Coverlet
L. 62 in   158 cm
W. 54 in   137 cm
Gift of Miss Mary H. Emerson

A fine example of Victorian needlework. Each silk hexagon is just $\frac{1}{2}$ in and the blue satin squares have been bordered with feather stitching. The border is gold coloured plush, and the backing gold satin. The coverlet was presented to Mrs William Brown Emerson of Boston and Brooklyn, New York when she was a young girl, by an elderly lady she called Aunt Maria. She cherished it so much that she kept it in a box and never used it.

New England
c 1865

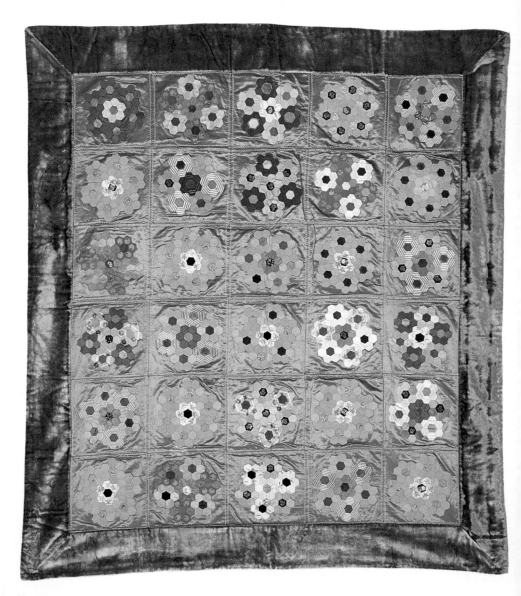

Grandmother's Flower Garden Quilt
L. 87 in   221 cm
W. 71 in   180 cm
Gift of Mrs Margaret Hildt

The Grandmother's Flower Garden pattern has been pieced from typical late Victorian silks, velvets and brocades. The backing is a green/pink shot silk and the mole coloured border is quilted beautifully in a running feather pattern. The quilt was made in Frederick, Maryland by Margaret Thomas, the donor's grandmother.

c 1870

**Dolly's Star
Quilt**
L. 102 in   260 cm
W. 107 in   265 cm

The simple eight-point star has been extended with eight further diamonds and the blocks have been set on point. The alternate white blocks have been quilted with flowers, foliage and fans. The shell border has been stuffed. In one block are the initials 'A.F.' and the date 1834 worked in corded quilting. Only a small portion of the quilt is shown here. The origin of the name is unknown.

Lancaster Co. Pennsylvania
1834

Star of Bethlehem Quilt
L. 104 in 264 cm
W. 100 in 254 cm

Well co-ordinated colours and neat piecing make this an outstanding example of a Star quilt. It is lightly padded and the quilting is neatly executed with outline quilting around the diamonds and shell quilting elsewhere.

Bethlehem, Pennsylvania
Nineteenth century

**Star
Quilt**
L. 108 in   272 cm
W. 104 in   261 cm
Gift of Mrs John Hanes

At the centre a large 8-point star made up of four double diamonds.
Four points of the star reach to the corners but the remaining four
at the sides of the quilt are cut short. The quilt is made of
multicoloured cottons and the seven inch border, white with a blue
sprig, has been appliqued with red flowers and green leaves.

Nineteenth century

Stars
Quilt
L. 102 in 259 cm
W. 83 in 211 cm
Gift of Mr W. A. Hardy

Multicoloured cottons make the stars on this quilt which has alternate white blocks. The four inch border is of red and white triangles. Each white square is quilted in a different pattern. The quilt has evidently been much used.

Inscribed in indelible ink on the back 'Sarah L. Smith, Yadre Le Magan from her Grandma, Sarah Rapelje, May 9th 1889'; members of Mr Hardy's wife's family.

Star and Crescent Quilt
L. 86 in 218 cm
W. 83 in 211 cm
Gift of Mrs R. T. Williams

This pattern is not often seen. The quilt has obviously been well used as the acid yellow fabric of the border is very worn. In some parts new material has been sewn over worn places in the half moon shaped segments. The quilting is outline round the piecing and zig zag on the sashing.

The donor's aunt was a Cornish woman who married a Cornish miner. They went to America where, like many other Cornishmen he found work. On their return to England they brought back this quilt.

Possibly 1930s

Stars and Octagons Quilt

L. 86 in 218 cm
W. 72 in 183 cm
Gift of Mr and Mrs Dunscombe Colt

Each block contains an eight-point star, the centre of which is a white octagon. Alternate blocks are white squares. The pattern can be looked at in several different ways and the placement of the diamond shapes is such that they also make cubes. Outline quilting. The use of octagons is unusual.

c 1850

Quilt
L. 93 in   237 cm
W. 88 in   226 cm

The sawtooth pattern has been pieced from a patterned cotton in shades of dark brown and dark green. This quilt has never been used and perhaps was made for a hope chest. On the white cotton backing is written in indelible ink 'I.R. Sterrett No. 8'. Cotton seeds have been left in the padding and the quilting in floral, leaf and feather patterns is very neat.

York Co., Pennsylvania
Nineteenth century

**Birds in the Air
Quilt**
L. 89 in   226 cm
W. 79 in   200 cm
Gift of Miss Doris Cotterell

This bedcover should be classed as a comforter as the padding is very thick cotton and the three layers have been tied not quilted. The backing is of the same material as the sashing.

c 1886

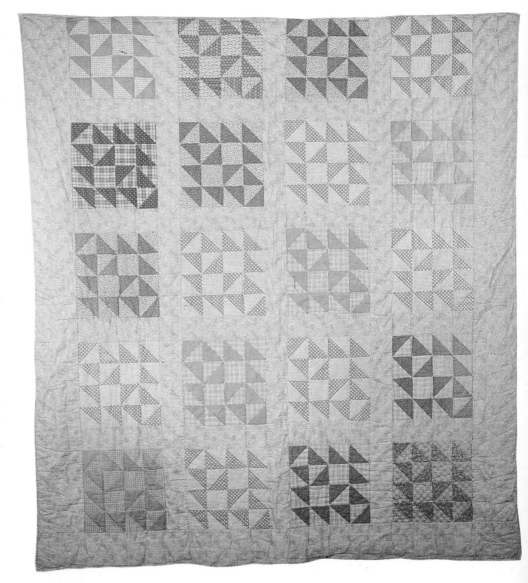

**Sawtooth
Quilt**
Square 94 in   239 cm

This pattern is also called Lend and Borrow, Lost Ships, Rocky Glen and Southern Mountains among others.

The triangles are cut from an acid green fabric which is printed with a very tiny black and red tree. Half a feather circle is quilted in the white part of the block. The quilt was made for Mrs Joanna Jones, née Clary.

Maryland
Mid nineteenth century

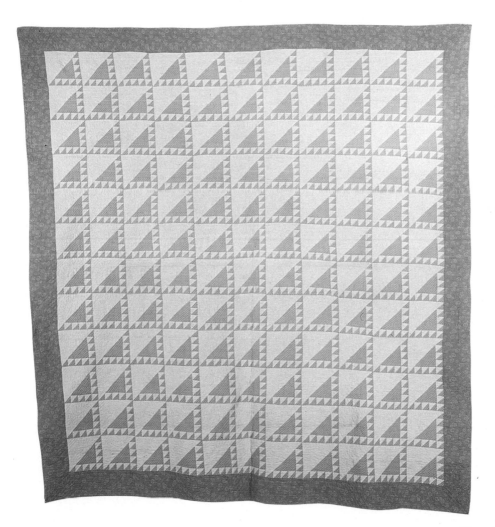

**New York Beauty
Quilt**
L. 78 in   198 cm
W. 68 in   175 cm
Gift of Mrs John D. Palmer

This pattern is sometimes called Crown of Thorns. The piecing is in red and yellow solid coloured fabric and the background is white with a small black dot. The quilting is outline around the pattern and diagonal elsewhere.

Early twentieth century

Sawtooth
Quilt
Square 82 in 210 cm
Gift of Mr and Mrs Robert Stolper

The sawtooth pattern has been made in red and blue cotton. The backing is a cream fabric printed with tiny red berries and faded green foliage. The quilting has been worked in patterns of feather roses, with diamonds. The red binding has been put on by sewing machine.

Second half nineteenth century

Lazy Rose
Quilt
L. 85 in   216 cm
W. 77 in   196 cm
Gift of Mrs Margaret Flower

The pink and white square pieced blocks are set on point so that the pattern is horizontal and vertical. There is a deliberate mistake in one of the blocks. The backing is white cotton and the quilting very neat with a rose variation in the solid white blocks and cable in the border.

Made by Margaret Camp Coss (donor's grandmother).

Possibly Ohio
c 1900

Baskets
Quilt
Square 84 in   213 cm
Gift of Miss Doris Cotterill

A version of the popular Baskets pattern. The pieced baskets have been assembled so that the centre row would sit at the middle of the bed and the remaining baskets would be the right way up seen from either side of the bed. The green applique hearts could mean that this was made as a marriage quilt. The quilting is very simple, outline, with floral motifs in the baskets.

Some of the fabrics are identical with those used for the Log Cabin quilt on pages 34 and 35 of 'Quilts and Coverlets' so this quilt could have been made by the same ladies, as it also came from the Cotterill family

c 1886

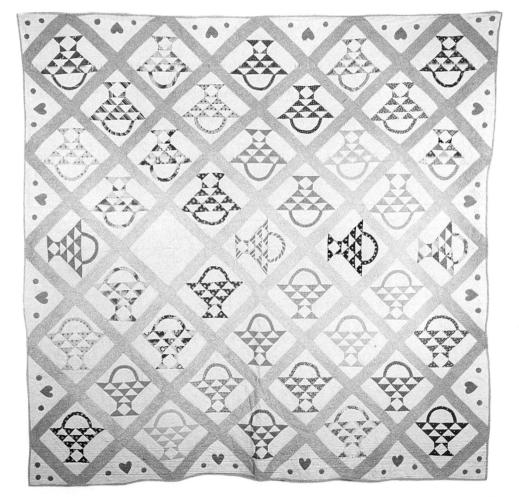

Meadow Lily
Quilt
Square 88 in   222 cm

The New York State version of the Lily pattern (see North Carolina Lily, Quilts and Coverlets page 53). The lilies have been made from two red and two yellow diamonds and a green triangle into 15 inch square blocks which have been given a sawtooth edge. The quilting pattern of roses and foliage has been finely worked over the whole surface of the quilt and bears no relation to the piecing.

Nineteenth century

Poinsettia
Quilt
L. 90 in   229 cm
W. 84 in   213 cm
Gift of Mrs Jason Westerfield

Another version of the Lily pattern. The quilting follows the piecing.
 Written on the back of the quilt, in indelible ink 'Made by Harriet Heddon, East Orange, New Jersey before 1856'.

Tumbling Blocks
Silk Patchwork
L. 66 in   168 cm
W. 60 in   153 cm
Gift of Mrs M. M. Young

From the size of this piece of work it would seem that it was made to put on the top of a bed as a decorative feature or to be used as a sofa 'throw'.

Second half nineteenth century

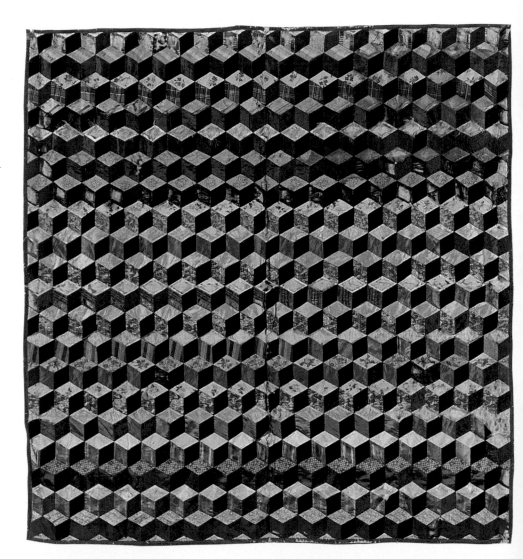

Fans
Quilt
L. 86 in   219 cm
W. 79 in   201 cm
*Gift of Beverly E. Williams and
Sara Leasure*

The pieced fans have been made from a wide variety of printed dress cottons. The square blocks are set on point and outline quilted.
There is a small triangle quilted in the point of each block. The quilt was made by Katy Clark Elmore of Chula, Missouri, grandmother and great grandmother of the donors.

1937

Double Wedding Ring Quilt
L. 84 in 213 cm
W. 70 in 178 cm
Gift of Mrs Jean Whittemore

The traditional blue and pink fabrics usually associated with the Double Wedding Ring pattern have been replaced by green and yellow. The piecing is very precise and the quilting in the white blocks very well executed.

Made by Mrs Margaret Whittemore (mother in law of the donor) for her son on the occasion of his marriage.

Colorado
1930

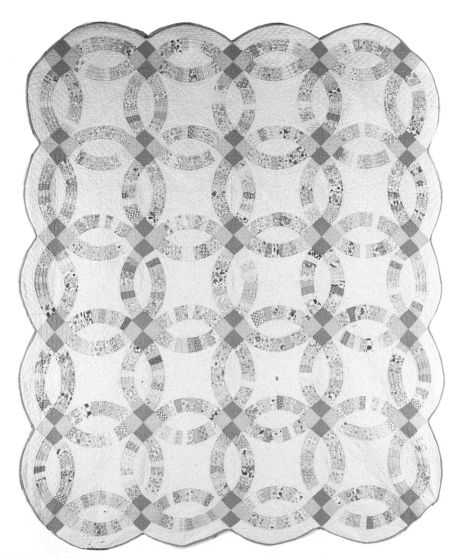

Double Wedding Ring Quilt
L. 96 in   246 cm
W. 70 in   178 cm
Gift of Mrs Sara Leasure

This Double Wedding Ring Quilt has been given a new dimension by the use of blue fabric, instead of the usual white, for the 'melon' shaped pieces.

The quilt was made by Katy Clark Elmore of Chula, Missouri from pieces left over from her daughter's (Beverley E. Williams) dresses. She was the donor's grandmother.

1935

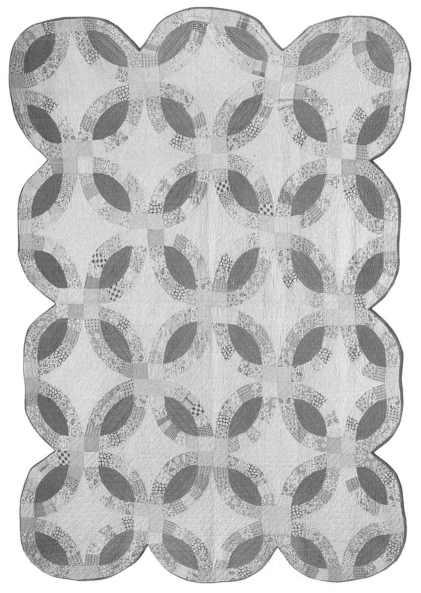

**Dresden Plate
Quilt**
L. 91 in   131 cm
W. 76 in   193 cm
Gift of Mrs Margaret Flower

The 'Dresden Plates' have been appliqued to a white background
and a single green leaf in the corner of each block contributes to a
secondary pattern. The border is attractive and unusual. Quilting is
outline round the 'plates' and chevron elsewhere. The quilt was
made by the donor's mother.

Possibly Ohio
c 1930

**Dresden Plate
Quilt**
L. 94 in   239 cm
W. 79 in   201 cm
Gift of Mrs Keith Mahan

The Dresden Plate pattern is one which allows many variations. Here the 'plates' have been appliqued to the block and a quilting pattern makes a feature of the intersection where the four blocks come together.

The top was pieced by hand by Marie Miller Farwell, the donor's mother, and quilted by the ladies of Northbrae Community Church, Berkeley, California.

1930s

Log Cabin Patchwork
L. 50 in   127 cm
W. 30 in   76 cm
Gift of Mr Howard D. Washburn

The variation of Log Cabin patchwork known as 'Pineapple' has been pieced of silk fabrics. The edge has been trimmed with 'tongues' also made of silk. The backing is gold silk, machine quilted, which was available commercially.

The patchwork was made by Mrs Ethelind Washburn, great grandmother of the donor.

1870s

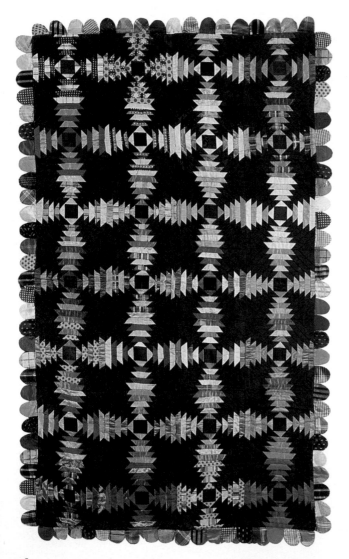

**Log Cabin
Coverlet**
Square 62 in   158 cm
Gift of Mrs Stephen Frink Dana

The Log Cabin blocks are made of silks and there is a dark maroon velvet border. The backing is a fine red woollen fabric and the coverlet has been 'tied' not quilted. Bows of narrow blue ribbon have been sewn over the knots on the reverse.

   This coverlet was made by Lucy Chapin Hawley (donor's grandmother), her sisters and mother from pieces from their dresses, while their father Daniel Chapin was away at the Civil War.

1860s

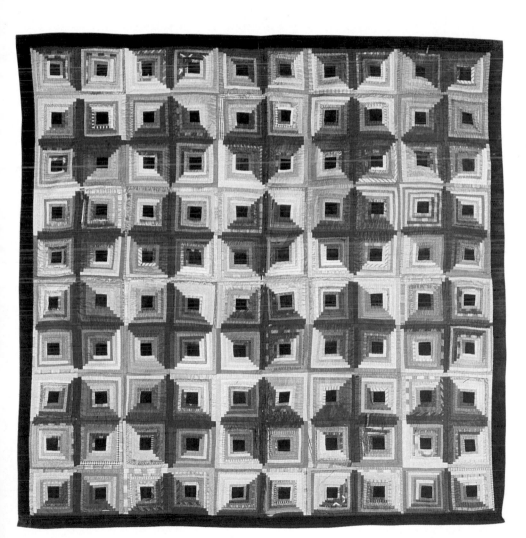

**Log Cabin
Coverlet**
L. 65 in   165 cm
W. 52 in   133 cm
Gift of Mrs Harriet Metcalf

Another coverlet in the Log Cabin pattern which has been made of silk fabrics. It is backed with grey silk. The coverlet was made by Mary E. Sexton Mann, who was born at Aurora, Illinois in 1823 and died *c* 1906. She was the donor's great grandmother.

Late nineteenth century

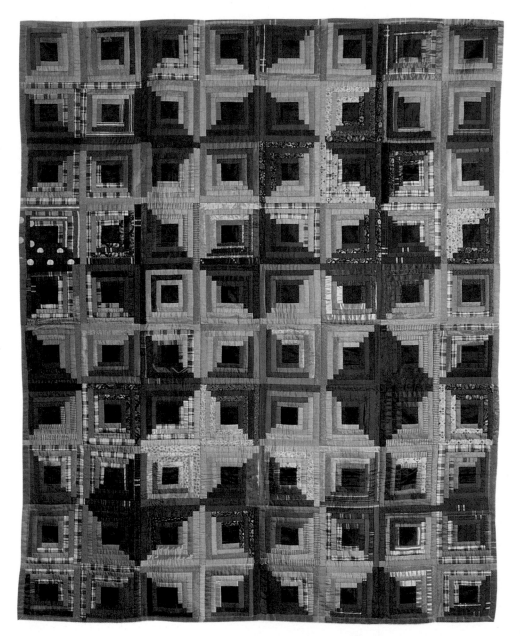

Log Cabin
Top only
L. 85 in   216 cm
W. 72 in   183 cm
Gift of Mrs Margaret Wylie
Sawbridge

Four Log Cabin blocks of silk fabrics make a ten inch block which is set on point. These blocks alternate with blocks cut from pink and beige striped silk. There is no backing and no quilting.

Late nineteenth century

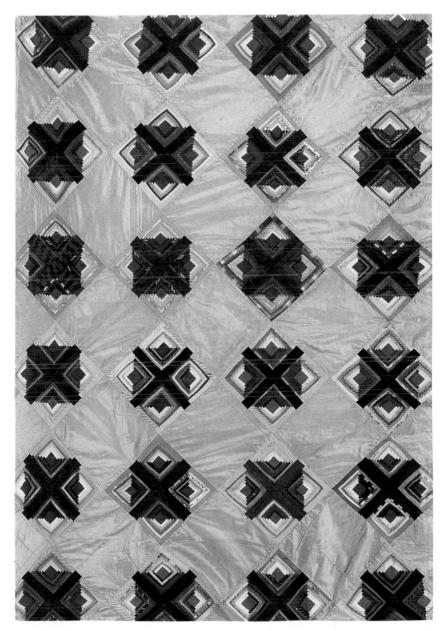

Log Cabin
Coverlet
L. 75 in   190 cm
W. 54 in   137 cm
Gift of Mrs Elizabeth Johnson

The Courthouse Steps variation of the Log Cabin pattern has been pieced of multi-coloured silks and has a beige silk backing. There is no quilting or padding.

It was made by Mrs Coates of Chester Heights, Pennsylvania who died at the age of 100 in 1913. She was the great great grandmother of the donor.

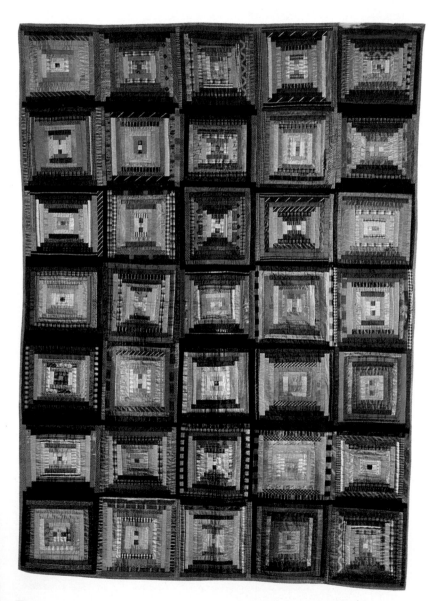

Chintz Medallion
Top only
Square 82 in   208 cm

At the centre is a 24 inch piece of chintz which has been surrounded by five borders. The sawtooth inner border has a rose in each of the corner squares. Some of the borders have been made from more than one piece of chintz.

c 1825

Strippy Quilt
L. 97 in   246 cm
W. 93 in   136 cm

Eight panels of brown sprigged cotton alternate with seven panels of white cotton. There is a ten inch white cotton border on three sides. The backing is a coarse homespun linen and the cotton filling has had some of the seeds left in. The leaves and swags and bows are outline quilted but the close quilting of the background gives the impression that they are stuffed. A commercial cotton fringe has been added on three sides. The initials E.I.D.A. have been printed on the reverse in marking ink.

Pennsylvania
c 1830

Strippy Quilt
L. 95 in 241 cm
W. 94 in 239 cm
Gift of Mrs Marion Channing

A very colourful example of a 'strippy quilt'. There are eight stripes blue with brown leaves and nine stripes red with yellow leaves alternating with eighteen stripes which have a pattern of sailors (wearing straw boaters) and anchors. The quilting is mainly diagonal.

c 1850

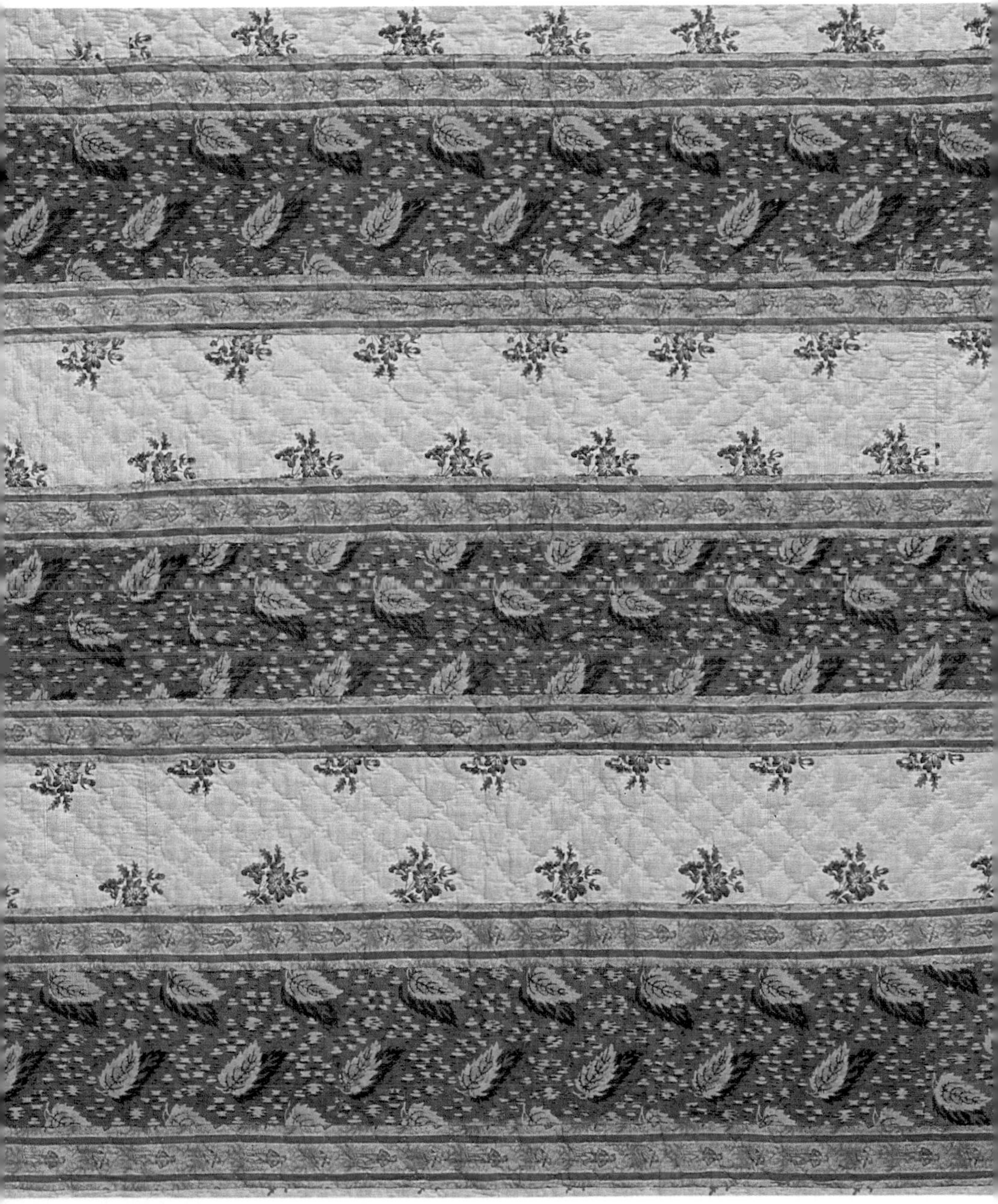

Amish Quilt
L. 86 in   218 cm
W. 72 in   184 cm

An Amish quilt pieced in typical mid west colours and fabrics. The beige, gold and tan fabrics are fine wool and the black is polished cotton. Tulips have been quilted in the black triangles and black border, hourglass quilting on beige, straight lines on pieced blocks and floral patterns on solid colour blocks. The backing is black cotton.

Milton, Iowa
1929
See 'Quilts and Coverlets' pp 41/43

Appliqué Quilts

Applied work or applique has a very long history and is known in many parts of the world. Crusaders wore surcoats on which emblems were embroidered, or applied, and in mediaeval times when textiles were scarce and expensive, pieces of rich woven fabric, too precious to throw away, were used as a substitute for embroidery by being sewn to the surface of another piece of cloth.

This same technique was used for some of the first appliqué bedcovers. Floral and bird motifs, often the best pieces left of Indian chintzes and palampores (cotton bedcovers) were cut out and sewn to a foundation material. The foundation itself often was made up of several pieces of fabric joined together.

The whole concept of an appliqué quilt is pictorial. The applique patterns on the top could make up one large design as in a painting, or smaller designs could be executed on blocks which were then joined together in the same way as pieced work. The appliqué patterns were often drawn freehand as in the many floral and leaf patterns. Abstract patterns could be made by the folded paper 'cut-out' process which was used to great effect in some Hawaiian designs.[1]

The 1920s and 1930s were years of great appliqué quilts. Led by such well-known American quilters as Marie Webster, Rose Kretsinger and Charlotte Jane Whitehill, women delighted in the pastel-coloured floral appliqué quilt patterns, many of which could be obtained commercially and were sold in kit form also. In order to give a three-dimensional effect to certain parts of the pattern, particularly flowers and buds, a padding of fine cotton was inserted beneath the applique shape.

It has often been said that pieced quilts were for everyday use and appliqué quilts were for best, but there seems little evidence to support this. The quilt maker herself designed her quilt in whichever medium she favoured and made it with whatever materials were available.

[1] S. Betterton, op. cit. pp 70, 71

Medallion Quilt
Square 82 in   208 cm
Gift of Dr John Cates

A medallion type quilt with a pillar print as the central motif. The inner border is a cheap American print of the 1840s. Flowers and birds cut from chintz and appliqued to a natural cotton foundation form the second border. The outer border is made from a number of pieces of chintz of the late eighteenth century. Because the outer border is of an earlier date than the inner one, the quilt must have been remade at some time. The backing is homespun and the bedcover is very closely quilted in diagonal lines and squares.

First quarter nineteenth century

Turkey Tracks Quilt
L. 89 in 227 cm
W. 84 in 214 cm

The central Turkey Tracks block is surrounded by five-point stars and six further Turkey Tracks Blocks. The border shows flowers, particularly tulips, also leaves and berries. The berries are stuffed. The quilting is random, scattered between appliques. There are many single motifs, abstract patterns leaves and hearts, so this may have been made as a marriage quilt.

Pennsylvania
Nineteenth century
See 'Quilts and Coverlets' p. 71

**Oak Leaves
Quilt**
L. 91 in   231 cm
W. 75 in   190 cm

The red and green colouring with white is typical of many nineteenth century quilts. This pattern has been cut with precision and carefully applied. The quilting in ribbon, leaf and flower patterns has been neatly worked. However, the maker seems to have had a little difficulty with her corners, but this does not detract from the charm of the quilt.

Lancaster Co., Pennsylvania
Nineteenth century

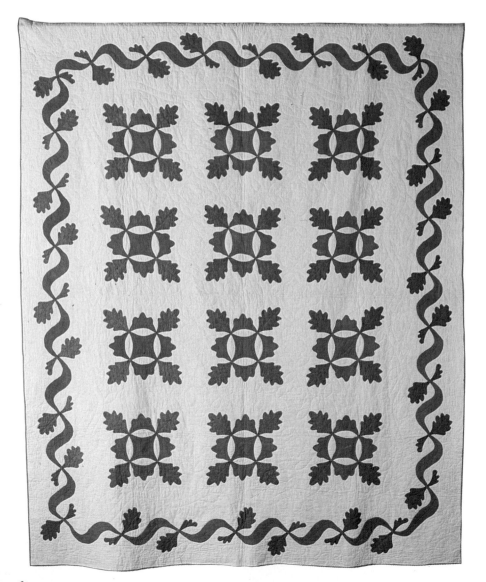

**Poinsettia
Quilt**
L. 92 in   234 cm
W. 82 in   208 cm

An attractive arrangement of poinsettia flowers and foliage in pots.
The applique is slightly stuffed. The quilting is simple but very neat,
diagonal over the whole top.

New Jersey
Nineteenth century

**Star, Dart and Feather
Quilt**
L. 79 in   201 cm
W. 76 in   193 cm

The red cotton pattern has been applied to a white ground. It has been meticulously cut out and sewn with very neat stitches. Chain quilting in the border.

Pennsylvania
Pre 1850

**Baseballs
Quilt**
L. 76 in   194 cm
W. 64 in   164 cm

Circles of patterned red or blue cotton 2½ inches diameter have been appliqued to squares of unbleached calico. The circles are surrounded with chain stitch worked in coarse cotton yarn and chain stitch is also worked diagonally across the intersections of the blocks. There is outline quilting round the circles and on either side of the chain stitch diagonals. Four hearts have been embroidered in the centre.

Cooperstown, New York State
Nineteenth century

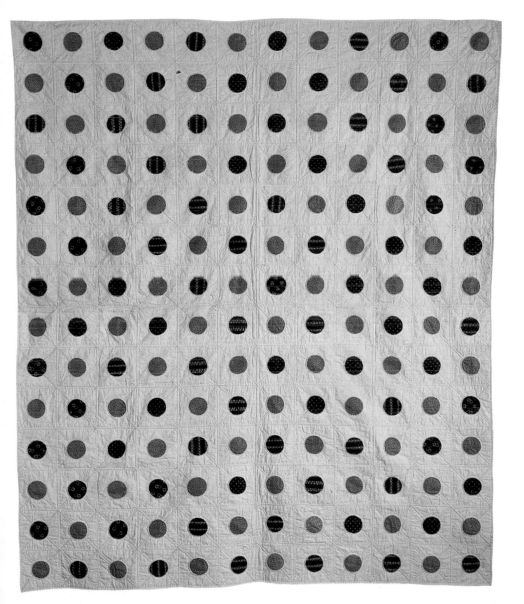

Wreath of Roses
Quilt
Square 82 in   208 cm

The Rose has always been a popular pattern for quilts. This is a simple interpretation very neatly worked, as were all quilts coming from Pennsylvania. The quilt shows the influence of the Turkey Red dye which reached America in the 1820s. The quilting is simple and neat, outline round the pattern and the background quilted diagonally overall.

Bucks Co., Pennsylvania
Nineteenth century

Wreath of Roses
Quilt
Square 78 in   200 cm

This quilt is made from two layers of material but the flowers and leaves have been stuffed to give texture to the surface. The swags and bows are also stuffed. Outline quilting round the applique with diagonal quilting in the sashing.

Mid nineteenth century

Princess Feather
Quilt
Square 88 in   223 cm

A rather unsophisticated version of the Princess Feather pattern. Contour quilting follows the outline of the feathers at one quarter inch intervals. See 'Quilts and Coverlets' pp 64/65.

Nineteenth century

Political Quilts

A number of quilt patterns have been given names associated with politics or history.

In the eighteenth and nineteenth centuries women had no vote and took no active part in politics, but they listened to what was being discussed and expressed their loyalty to a political party in the naming of quilt patterns. Only two commemorate British participation in America's history. The pattern 'Queen Charlotte's Crown' was named for the wife of King George III, who was the last Queen of America before Independence. 'Burgoyne Surrounded' commemorates General Burgoyne, who was defeated at the Battle of Saratoga in 1777.

Some patterns were named for Presidents or their wives; for example 'Dolly Madison Star' after the wife of the fourth President, and 'Mrs Cleveland's Choice' named for the beautiful girl who became the wife of President Grover Cleveland. Statesmen such as Henry Clay ('Clay's Choice'), Abraham Lincoln ('Lincoln's Platform') and Stephen A. Douglas ('The Little Giant') are remembered, as well as William Henry Harrison, ninth President of the United States and his Vice President John Tyler, with the pattern 'Tippecanoe and Tyler Too'.

The rose is featured in such patterns as 'Whig Rose' and 'Democrat Rose'. In 1782 Congress adopted the eagle as an emblem of the Great Seal of the United States and it became a very popular design motif. Not only was it woven into textiles and appliqued on to quilts but it was used on furniture, glass and porcelain. The eagle as a design motif went out of fashion during the 1840s but was revived at the time of the Civil War when it was known as the 'Union' pattern. It was used mainly by quiltmakers in the north and particularly in Pennsylvania. At this time the eagles were arranged diagonally across the corners of the work. The eagle was used again briefly at the time of the Philadelphia Centennial Exposition in 1876 and flags and patriotic sayings were often included in the design.

During the 1930s a number of quilts were made depicting a donkey which represented the Democrat party or an elephant for the Republican party.

**Tippecanoe and Tyler Too
Quilt**
L. 80 in   203 cm
W. 74 in   188 cm
Gift of Mrs John Haverstock

There has been an error in the making of this quilt or perhaps the maker could not quite get all her star blocks to fit together. Fabrics can be dated 1800, 1810 and 1815 and the border is an English chintz of the 1820s. The quilting is an all-over pattern of fans. The backing is an American printed fabric depicting President Elect William Harrison, a Whig, and his running mate for Vice President, John Tyler during the 1840 presidential campaign. It shows the slogan 'Harrison and Reform' under a likeness of the hero of the Indian battle of Tippecanoe with the log cabin and cider barrel which was supposed to exemplify the homespun simplicity of the candidate as against the alleged extravagance of his aristocratic opponent, Van Buren, a Democrat.

c 1840

Whig Rose Quilt

L. 94 in   239 cm
W. 92 in   232 cm

The stylised rose was adopted by the American Whig Party, formed in the 1830s to oppose the Democrats, as one of its emblems. It is best remembered for the colourful Presidential campaign of William Henry Harrison in 1840 (see Page 68).

The quilting is free and flowing in running feather and feather circle patterns.

The quilt was made in the early nineteenth century and comes from New York State.

**Union
Quilt**
L. 79 in   200 cm
W. 76 in   193 cm

This Union quilt has eagles made of red, yellow and grey cotton applied to an orange ground. The centre star is green and the border striped green, orange and red. The attractive backing is of black cotton with a small rose pattern and in the centre of the quilt this backing shows through because some of the filling is missing. The border is cable quilted and the background fabric is hatched in diamond quilting.

c 1880s

Album Quilts

An Album Quilt is a co-operative effort. Each of the many squares is made by a different individual or group of friends in honour of the person to whom the quilt is to be presented. The squares are often signed and dated, and usually included motifs relevant to the recipient's life and interests.

Under the general heading of Album Quilts are 'Presentation' Quilts, 'Friendship' Quilts, 'Bride's' Quilts and 'Freedom' Quilts. A quilt where each block contains a different pattern is called a 'Friendship Medley' quilt.

Quilts were often made to be presented to a Minister of Religion, perhaps on his leaving the parish or as a mark of respect. They were made for respected members of the community, the motifs often illustrating events in their life and work. A 'Freedom' quilt could be made for a young man on reaching the age of 21. His sisters and girl friends pieced the top for him, which he then put away until he became engaged. Then he gave the top to his future bride to be counted as one of the dozen quilts which she was hoping to make.

One quilting story suggests that after a girl's engagement had been announced, a friend or relative would arrange a Friendship Medley surprise party. Each guest was responsible for making her own block whilst the hostess provided the materials to set the blocks together. The girl for whom the party was given would then invite the same friends to a quilting bee when the top was ready to be made into a quilt.

The most sophisticated of all Album quilts are those which were made in Baltimore between 1843 and 1853[1] by a group of women who worked through the Methodist Church.

Towards the end of the nineteenth century Album quilts were made by schoolgirls and the signatures provided a record of all the girls in a particular class.

Bible or Scripture quilts were made, on which religious verses were inked or embroidered on each block, usually in red yarn. During two World Wars the Red Cross and other groups organised the making of Album quilts. Interested persons paid a small sum of money to have their name embroidered on the quilt top and the finished quilt was sold or raffled for a good cause.

[1] S. Betterton, op. cit., pp. 80/82.

Friendship Quilt
Square 99 in   251 cm

Red and white patterned calicos make eight-point stars alternating with solid white squares and circles. Many of the white fabrics are signed and dated. The quilting is very simple. In the detail shown it is just possible to make out the inscription 'Made in Crescent City, Maryland as a Friendship offering to Mr How by the ladies of St George's Church, 1847.'

Friendship Quilt
L. 94 in   239 cm
W. 101 in   256 cm

The quilt is composed of 72 blocks most of which have been signed. The background is white with red, blue and green applique patterns while the 6 inch border has green swags with red drops and bows. The quilting follows the pattern in the blocks and border and is diagonal on the sashing.

New Paltz, New York State
1851

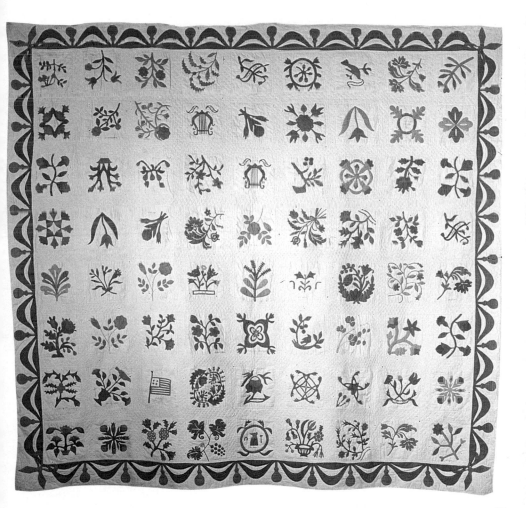

Friendship Quilt
L. 80 in   204 cm
W. 78 in   200 cm

Each of the forty nine blocks making up the quilt top are eight inches square. At the centre of each block is a white square on which the name of the maker has been written in indelible ink. The backing is a brown patterned cotton and the quilting very simple, just diagonal lines four inches apart. Quilts such as this were often made by a class of schoolgirls.

Late nineteenth century

Slave Quilts

Many of the black slaves brought to America from the west coast of Africa were skilled craftspeople, and they brought with them a knowledge of basket-making, pottery, woodcarving, netting, weaving and a form of needlework.

In the early years of colonisation there was a need for craftspeople and there was a big demand for spinners and weavers. These skills brought high prices when slaves were being sold. Slaves who showed an aptitude for needlework eventually were trained to do all kinds of tasks, such as tatting, embroidery, knitting and dressmaking, as well as the plain sewing needed for patchwork and quilting. They made all the household textiles for the slaves as well as for the family.

White women who opposed slavery used their needlework to draw attention to anti-slavery campaigns. Bazaars and fairs organised by both white and free black women raised funds for such campaigns. Conversely there were others who used patchwork and quilting to support slavery.

The two slave-made quilts in the museum's collection reflect the deliberate instructions of the slave owners, and are quite different from quilts designed by the black women themselves. The coverlet top which was made on the Drayton Hall plantation in South Carolina is meticulously pieced from hexagons only one half-inch across, the motifs then being applied to a cream cotton background. Each hexagon has been cut so that the motif, strawberry, nut or bud, is in the exact centre.

Many quilts designed by black women can be identified by strip piecing, together with bright colours and large patterns which are often asymmetrical. The makers often improvise and can give to a European or white American pattern their own individual interpretation.

Coverlet
L. 130 in 330 cm
W. 112 in 285 cm

A coverlet 'top' which has never been backed or quilted. Each $\frac{1}{2}$ in hexagon has been cut so that the bud or flower is exactly in the centre. The border is chintz and the bands dividing the applique motifs are printed cotton. A note attached to the coverlet says that it was made by negro sempstresses on the family plantation (Drayton Hall), South Carolina.

Early nineteenth century

Chalices
Quilt
L. 87 in   221 cm
W. 75 in   191 cm
Gift of Mrs W. Webster Downer

Thirty white blocks with applique motif representing a chalice alternate with solid red blocks. The backing is red and white striped cotton and arcs have been quilted in white thread over the whole surface of the quilt. The chalices represent the Bishop who visited the Mimosa Hall Plantation in Texas once a year.

Family legend tells that the Anglican Bishop from New Orleans came once a year to baptise, confirm and marry. He stayed with different families on the many cotton plantations in the area. It was the custom to make a new quilt for the Bishop's use each time he visited. Everyone helped including children and slaves. Because the workmanship was not particularly fine the quilts were usually used after the Bishop's visit by the children or the house servants.

c 1860

Sioux Indian Quilts

It was the duty of the Sioux Indian women of the western plains to provide the clothing and household needs of their family. Skins and other animal products furnished almost all their needs, besides the materials of their native art. Women did the sewing and decorated their work with paint, seeds, shells, animal teeth, quills and of course, beads of all kinds. Men painted realistic figures such as birds, animals and humans, while women painted only geometric forms which were also used in the quill and bead embroidery. So the Sioux Indian woman was able to adapt very readily to the disciplined and geometric forms of patchwork when introduced to them by white women.

The Sioux had no knowledge of sewing cloth with needle and thread until taught by the white women, but have since learnt to sew by hand and to use the sewing machine. This is a comparatively recent skill which helps the Indian women produce something which is marketable. However, although they are using white women's techniques, their quilts still show the bold colours and the sharp angular outlines which are characteristic of the Indian.

One of the most popular patterns is the Star, particularly the 'Lone Star'. Among the Sioux tribes a period of mourning after a death lasts for one year, after which relatives celebrate with a Sioux 'giveaway', a Lakota memorial service for the dead. One custom at this time is to display the finest quilts, which are then presented to friends who have been kind to the decreased during his or her lifetime. The most common and cherished gift is a 'Lone Star' pattern quilt. As it is a Sioux tradition not to copy either from tradition or a neighbour, but for each quilter to create her own beauty, many of these depart slightly from the basic pattern. The quilts are pieced on the sewing machine and the quilting, which is usually quite simple, is worked by hand.

The Museum is fortunate to have three Sioux Indian quilts in the permanent collection.

**Lone Star
Quilt**
L. 78 in   199 cm
W. 64 in   164 cm
Gift of Miss Dorothy Dignam

The Star pattern has been pieced by sewing machine from cotton fabrics in bright colours. In contrast the backing is a white fleecy material printed with dainty floral motifs. The quilting is very simple and rather large stitches have been used. The quilt was made by an Indian woman from the Wounded Knee Trading Post.

1973

**Lone Star
Quilt**
L. 89 in   226 cm
W. 76 in   193 cm

A Lone Star pattern quilt which incorporates the Cheyenne tipi into the points of the star. In the centre the applique war bonnet has white feathers tipped with black. Blue wool has been tufted for other feathers and the ribbons are free. The quilting is outline with shell in the background. The quilt was made by Margaret Little Thunder, a Sioux Indian, at Crazy Horse in the Black Hills of South Dakota.

1983

Lone Star
Quilt
Square 84 in   213 cm

The Lone Star pattern is a favourite with Sioux Indian women. In this instance the maker has used the strong colours typical of Plains Indian decoration. The central star is 'tied', there is a quilted star in each corner and the border is chevron quilted. The quilt has been pieced on a sewing machine and hand quilted. The outline of a Cheyenne tipi has been incorporated into the points of the star.

The Black Hills, South Dakota
1983

Crazy Patchwork

About the middle of the nineteenth century a new style of patchwork emerged. It was called crazy patchwork; crazy meaning cracked or crazed as used in the term crazy paving. Godey's Lady's Book, one of the most popular women's magazines of the day advertised kits for making crazy patchwork as early as 1855 but the technique did not reach the height of its popularity until after about 1870 and it lasted over into the early 1900s.

It was at this time that the 'decorative art' craze swept America and women were encouraged to experiment with new aesthetic styles and ideas in decorating, partly owing to the aesthetic movement of Ruskin and Morris. Decorative Art Societies influenced quiltmaking from about 1876 to 1893, by promoting new types of bedcovers and rejecting cotton patchwork. Patchwork fell under the heading of plain sewing rather than fancy work. Calico squares were considered helpful for teaching little girls to sew, but making crazy patchwork became socially acceptable, and crazy quilts were made to be shown off as works of art. Furthermore, after the rigors of the War between the States women felt that they needed an outlet which would cheer up their homes and give them a satisfying hobby at the same time.

Most crazy patchwork was made of rich fabrics; silks, brocades, velvets and silk ribbons, cut in random shapes which were basted to a background cloth, the seams then being covered with intricate embroidery. Women vied with each other to see how much embroidery they could use. Herringbone stitch was the most popular but many of the stitches were not to be found in any embroidery book and were original to the individual needle-woman. Narrow 'China' ribbons were employed instead of embroidery floss to work floral sprays and borders. Flowers and birds were often painted on some of the pieces, and in some cases even photographs were incorporated into the work.

These pieces of crazy patchwork could be worked in blocks as in cotton patchwork or could be made up in one piece, and were seldom put to use as bedcovers. Those that were made as coverlets were inclined to be smaller than usual, so that they lay on top of the bed and enabled the whole creation to be admired. This technique was employed to make portieres, mats for the dressing table or mantelshelf, covers for tables or 'throws' to grace the arm of a sofa or piano, as well as for beds.

Crazy Patchwork
L. 69 in   175 cm
W. 55 in   139 cm
Gift of Mrs Fanny E. Edwards

Crazy patchwork in silks and brocades. The backing is a maroon coloured fleecy material and the whole is thickly padded. There is no quilting. The scalloped edge is made of silk

Late nineteenth century

Crazy Patchwork
Square 66 in   168 cm
Gift of Mrs Elizabeth Frost

This is an outstanding example of crazy patchwork. The fabrics are silks, velvets, brocades and ribbons, all heavily embroidered. Some flowers have been painted on and others worked in ribbons. The wedge-shaped border is made of grey silk and black velvet. It was made by Mary Elizabeth Plowman Kschinka, grandmother of the donor in Fort Leavenworth, Kansas. Mary Elizabeth's father was Judge Thomas Plowman of Baltimore, Maryland, who, after the Civil War was posted to Kansas. On his trips back to Baltimore he would buy silks and other dress fabrics for his wife and daughters and this 'throw' has been made from the scraps left over.

Last quarter nineteenth century

**Crazy Patchwork
Quilt**
L. 86 in   219 cm
W. 68 in   173 cm
Gift of Mrs C. Buck Churchman

Thickly padded bedcovers which were 'tied' rather than quilted were usually called 'comforters'. This comforter has been made from a random selection of scraps and pieces left over from dressmaking and includes a 'Domino' sugar bag. It is thickly padded and is backed with a grey, striped flannel backing.

Early twentieth century

88

Crib and Doll Quilts

The practice of making small-size bed-coverings for children's cots goes back in America to the seventeenth century and continues to the present day. Sizes and shapes vary considerably because there were many different types of beds in which infants were put to sleep.

Some quilts were pieced like full-sized quilts[1] but on a much smaller scale, whilst others were made of whole cloth, often white, intricately quilted.

Doll quilts were made either by the mother or by the child herself, who might learn her patchwork and quilting skills on these small pieces of work. Again, sizes vary, no doubt as a result of the different sizes of doll's furniture.

'The American Girl's Book', published in 1831, suggests, 'Little girls often find amusement in making patchwork quilts for the beds of their dolls, and some even go so far as to make cradle quilts for their infant brothers and sisters.'

[1] S. Betterton, op. cit pp. 24, 25.

Quilt
Square $14\frac{1}{2}$ in   37 cm

Five strips of red and white cotton have been sewn alternately with four strips of plain white. There is little padding and the diamond quilting has been done on the sewing machine.

The quilt belonged to a Quaker family, the Bailey family of Pottstown, Westchester Co., Pennsylvania.

Second half nineteenth century

The miniature 'field' bed is just 20 inches long and 13 inches wide. The arched tester has a modern copy of a nineteenth century netted canopy. The doll which is only $9\frac{1}{2}$ in high is made of papier mache and wood and is covered with a piece of homespun and a small 'strippy' quilt.

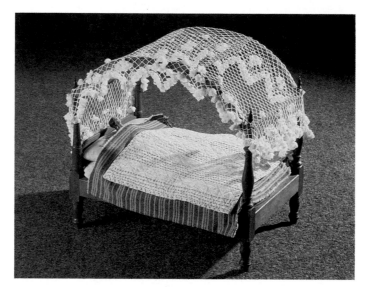

Quilt
L. 30 in   76 cm
W. 16 in   41 cm
Gift of Mrs Emerin Chute

Log Cabin pattern doll quilt made mainly in shades of pink and blue cotton

Late nineteenth century

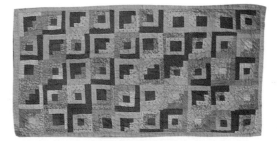

Quilt
L. 17½ in   44 cm
W. 8½ in   22 cm
Gift of Mrs Marian Channing

A small quilt probably made for a doll's cradle. The pattern 'Flying Geese' has been pieced from white together with a very dark green patterned cotton. The backing is natural colour which has a tiny black motif and the quilting is in diagonal lines which bears no relation to the piecing. *c* 1875

Quilt
L. 20½ in   52 cm
W. 19½ in   50 cm
Gift of Mrs Paul Abbott

Pieced by hand of one inch multicoloured cotton squares. The three borders each have a square of chintz in the corners. The backing is white cotton which has a red sprig and the bedcover is quilted overall in a diamond pattern.

The quilt was made by Catherine Wilfe of New York State who married George Bruce in 1811.

Cot Quilt
L. 48 in   122 cm
W. 42 in   107 cm
*Gift of Mrs Margaret Wylie
Sawbridge*

This all white cotton cot quilt is an example of exquisite needlework. The quilting is beautifully worked, diagonal in the middle with a feather pattern border of stuffed work. The quilt is lightly padded and some of the cotton seeds have been left in

c 1810

This cot quilt belonged to Judge Andrew Wylie who died in 1901 aged 92 years. He was a Justice of the District of Columbia Supreme Court and played a large part in the trial of Mary Garratt, who hid John Wilkes Booth after he had assassinated Abraham Lincoln. Judge Wylie and his wife Mary Caroline Bryan were the grandparents of the donor.

**Ohio Star
Crib Quilt**
Square 38 in   96 cm
Gift of Mrs Margaret Flower

Sixteen blocks each $4\frac{1}{2}$ inches square have been pieced in the red and white Ohio Star pattern. They alternate with solid colour white blocks which are diagonally quilted. The six inch white border is feather quilted and the edge bound in red.

The quilt was made by Elenora Campbell Camp of Wayne Co., Ohio (donor's great grandmother) for Margaret Jane Camp Coss (donor's grandmother)

1856

The Quilting Frame

The basic quilting frame consists of two long wooden bars called rails and two shorter flat pieces of wood called stretchers. The stretchers fit into slots in the rails and are held in place by wooden pegs. Each rail has a piece of braid or webbing attached to its inner edge.

Generally, each end of this frame would rest on the top of a straight-backed chair so that the frame could be easily stowed away when sewing for the day was finished. Sometimes the frame rested on trestles, and in the mountain areas of eastern Kentucky and eastern Tennessee, a frame, the full size of the quilt, is lowered from the ceiling by rope and pulley when quilting is to begin. At the end of the day the quilt is hauled up to the ceiling once again.

The quilting frame in the Museum's collection is unusual in that the trestles on which it stands are an integral part of the frame. Ratchets at one end hold the quilt firmly in place. Quilting frames of this type are very rare.

If the quilting is to be done by a number of women then a square frame with a trestle at each corner is often used. The whole quilt can then be put in the frame, and as the work progresses the trestles can be moved in and the quilt rolled on to make the centre of the work more accessible.

The method of working is the same whichever type of frame is used. The three layers are tacked together then all three layers are tacked to the webbing on the rails and are rolled on together, leaving a piece of fabric about two feet wide on which to sew. As the work progresses the quilt is wound on to the front rail, thus exposing an unsewn stretch of fabric.

Quilting is the last process in the making of a quilt, tying together the applique or pieced top, the filling and the backing with a design sewn in running stich.

Children's Quilts

Each year thousands of school children visit the museum in organised parties. Although some visits form part of pleasant outings, most are prepared for and followed up in a carefully co-ordinated educational programme.

It is sometimes difficult to judge what impression the Museum has made. This makes it gratifying when schools send examples of the work which has resulted from a visit. The children of three primary schools have put together hangings showing which objects in the museum's collection impressed them most during their own visit.

Wall Hanging
L. 76 in   193 cm
W. 73 in   185 cm
*Gift of Class 3, Weston Zoyland
Primary School*

Album type coverlet or wall hanging, each block 12 in. square made
by 8 and 9-year old pupils of Weston Zoyland County Primary
School, Somerset after a visit to the American Museum in Britain.
Blocks represent all aspects of life within the United States of
America and each child has signed his or her block.

1983

Wall Hanging
L. 90 in   228 cm
W. 76 in   193 cm
Gift of Class 1, Dauntsey's Primary
School

Album type coverlet or wall hanging made by 9 to 11 year-old pupils
of Dauntsey's Primary School, West Lavington, Wiltshire. The
blocks have been sewn to a backing which has been tie-dyed. The
children have chosen objects from the Museum's collection and have
used a great deal of imagination in transferring them into the applique
blocks. The Indian girl's plaits are made of braided wool and the war
bonnet has real feathers and ribbons.

1986

Wall Hanging
L. 76 in   188 cm
W. 44 in   112 cm
Gift of Minchinhampton Primary
School, Gloucestershire

Felt has been used throughout for the applique patterns. Each block has been outlined with red machine stitching. An interesting detail is the use of applique leaves at the intersections of the blocks.

1985

All-White Bedcovers

Bedcovers made entirely in white were at the height of their popularity between about 1790 and 1830. They were made for decorative purposes rather than warmth and suited the Greek Revival and Empire styles of furnishings which were fashionable at the time.

There were several types of all-white bedcovers. Quilted bedcovers seldom had an interlining but were made with a top of fine linen and a backing which was a coarser fabric. Several techniques might be employed in one piece work; corded quilting, in which a cord ran between two parallel rows of stiching, and stuffed work or trapunto which raised parts of the design into relief. The background could be closely stipple quilted. The term trapunto does not appear in American documents of the seventeenth, eighteen or early nineteenth centuries although stuffing and cording in needlework were well known in colonial America. Trapunto is a modern term for a very much older technique. To make an all-white bedcover its beauty depending entirely on the stichery, presented a far greater challenge to the needlewoman than the making of one of patchwork.

In the south white linen or cotton was embroidered, many of the designs being associated with crewel embroidery, particularly the "Tree of Life" patterns. These coverlets were not textured and the embroidery lay flat on the surface of the cloth. Many different embroidery stiches were employed including French and bullion knots, chain, satin and outline stiches and couching. This white embroidery on white was known as "white work" and was not confined to bedcovers. Other household items and articles of clothing were made from white work.

Other all-white coverlets were known as Candlewick bed spreads because the yarn used was a cotton roving, an inexpensive type of twisted cotton, similar to that which was used to make the wicks of candles. Some the spreads were embroidered with the candlewick cotton, mainly in French knots with a light weight roving, a heavier type being employed for the laid and couched work. Other stitches were sometimes used and a tufted effect could be achieved by clipping the stitches.

Candlewick coverlets were also made on the loom, the pattern being obtained by raising the weft with a stick or wire to leave small loops on the surface of the work. The reverse is smooth. The geometric patterns on some of the woven candlewick coverlets are very similar to those produced in Bolton, Lancashire for over two hundred years and which were known as "caddow" or "caddy" quilts. Great numbers were produced for export and were imitated in Canada and in the United States where coverlets made in the Rutger's factory in Patterson, New Jersey show strong Bolton influence.

Apart from geometric patterned bedcovers, patterns on most white spreads tend to be similar having a basket, urn or pot of flowers as the central motif, floral or geometric borders and other fruit or floral motifs in the four corners.

Some of the all-white coverlets were fringed; with a self fringe; with a commercially manufactured fringe, or on many early coverlets, a netted fringe. Netting was extremely popular in America during the eighteenth and nineteenth centuries and was one of the accomplishments included in the needlework teaching of the early finishing schools.

White work of all kinds was used for crib and cot quilts which were often with a netted fringe, similar to that used for full-sized quilts and bedcovers.

Candlewick Coverlet
L. 98 in   249 cm
W. 87 in   221 cm

The foundation material is a ribbed weave, made in three breadths, two of 35 in and one of 17 in joined together. The pattern of a central basket surrounded with an octagonal feather pattern border has been embroidered with thick candlewick cotton. Other motifs and the geometric outer border have been embroidered with the same cotton.

A fringe has been added to three sides
1820/40

Candlewick Coverlet
L. 92 in   233 cm
W. 87 in   221 cm
Gift of Miss Mary Allis

The foundation material is homespun linen and the pattern has been embroidered with candlewick cotton. The flowers such as the dianthus and tulip echo the patterns of crewel embroidery and the vase is out of proportion compared with the very large flowers.

A fringe has been added on three sides
1820/40

Candlewick Coverlet
L. 105 in   267 cm
W. 93 in   236 cm

In this instance the candlewick pattern has been woven into the background fabric. The coverlet looks unfinished with one side lacking a border and having a corner cut out – perhaps to accommodate a bed post near a wall. The swags and drops are similar to patterns used on many quilts.

The initials 'M.E.' have been embroidered on the coverlet.
Pennsylvania
Nineteenth century

A view of a bedroom from New Orleans at the middle of the
nineteenth century. The ornately carved mahogany bed is 6 ft. 8 in.
long and 6 ft. wide. The half tester is lined with quilted ivory satin.
The coverlet is a fine example of quilting, corded quilting and stuffed
work with a netted fringe. The window curtains are of tambour
embroidered muslin.

Coverlet
L. 102 in   259 cm
W. 96 in   244 cm

Three breadths natural coloured linen have been joined to make the background for the coverlet. The central design of cornucopia, leaves and flowers is all of stuffed work and is surrounded by stuffed flowers, leaves and acorns with a border of fronds in stuffed work. The stuffed oval shapes in the outer border give a rope-like effect.

Closely worked diagonal quilting covers the whole of the background. An 11 in. netted fringe has been added to three sides. There is an almost indecipherable inscription embroidered on the coverlet '... Cragin(?) from her grandmother'

c 1825

Woven Coverlets

Diaries kept by young American girls during the eighteenth and nineteenth centuries reveal that they spent a great deal of time spinning, weaving and sewing. The whole family depended upon them and their mother for all its textile needs. It was appreciated that a textile industry should be established but this was not possible until after the war of Independence when America was freed from British restrictions.

All girls were taught in the home to weave simple patterns in 'tabby' weave, under and over as in darning. The over-shot weave where the weft floated over several threads of the warp could also be woven in the home. However, because of limitations of the loom, patterns were always geometric. For more complicated patterns the home weaver usually needed skilled assistance. The patterns, called 'drafts' were narrow strips of paper which recorded a series of straight lines, dots and dashes – the codes by which the design was woven. The drafts were kept rolled and traditionally tied with black thread.

Early in the nineteenth century the French inventor, Joseph Marie Jacquard (1752–1834) invented an attachment for the loom which enabled more elaborate designs to be woven and after 1820 when this invention reached America, patterns underwent a radical change. Also about this time large numbers of skilled weavers emigrated to America from Scandinavia, Germany and Scotland. After working for some time in the east many moved further west to Ohio, Indiana, Illinois and Iowa. These Jacquard weavers were professionals and in many instances the weaver would incorporate his name or initials, the date, often the name of a town, and sometimes the name of the person for whom the coverlet was being woven into his piece of work.

The great years of coverlet weaving ended with the Civil War, after which factory made blankets became cheap and plentiful. Old spinning and weaving skills began to die out but the original methods of production remained in general use in the south particularly in the isolated areas of Tennessee and Kentucky, far longer than they did in the north. While traditionally made coverlets were still being woven in Kentucky until the 1930s a similar product from New England would have had to be made earlier than 1850, because by that time much textile production had already been taken over by machinery.

Blankets
L. 86 in   219 cm
W. 63 in   160 cm

Two homespun woollen blankets embroidered in crewel wools of blue, red and yellow.

Greenfield, Massachusetts
Early nineteenth century

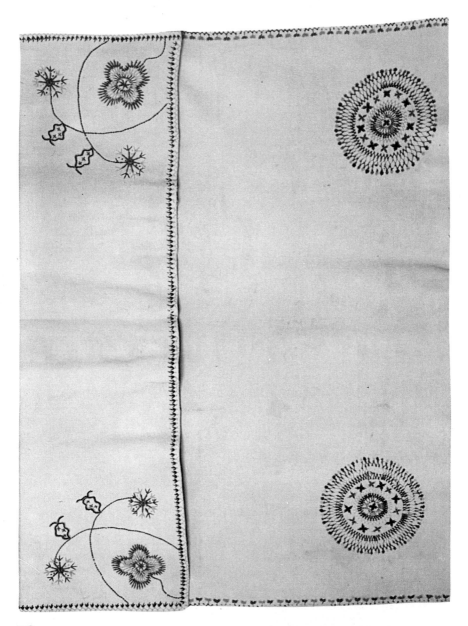

Blanket
L. 91 in   231 cm
W. 80 in   203 cm
Gift of Miss Nancy Hay

Indigo blue and natural wool blanket which has been woven in two pieces and joined. The pattern and colours are typical of many homespun and home woven covers.

c 1860

Woven Coverlet
L. 80 in   203 cm
W. 68 in   173 cm
Gift of Miss Nancy Hay

Overshot weave coverlet in a pattern known sometimes as 'Nine Snowballs' which has been woven in two sections and joined. The warp is natural linen and the weft red and green wool. There is a fringe on three sides

c 1820

Woven Coverlet
L. 87 in   221 cm
W. 84 in   213 cm
Gift of Mr Edward Wormley

The coverlet has been woven in two pieces and joined. Both warp and weft are of natural, pale blue and indigo blue wool. There are fringes on three sides and the fourth side is bound. This technique is sometimes called 'Summer and Winter' weave because the method of weaving produces a dark pattern on one side (for winter) and a light pattern on the reverse (for summer).

Early nineteenth century

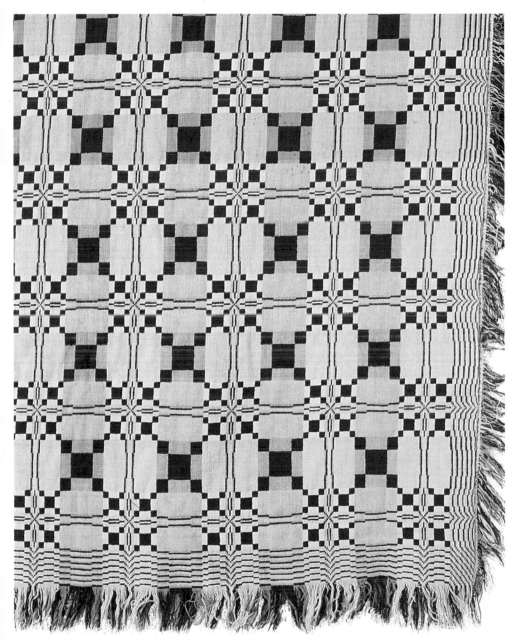

Woven Coverlet
L. 85 in   213 cm
W. 74 in   188 cm
Gift of Miss Nancy Hay

This coverlet has been woven in two pieces, and joined, of a natural cotton warp with a tan and indigo blue weft.

Nineteenth century

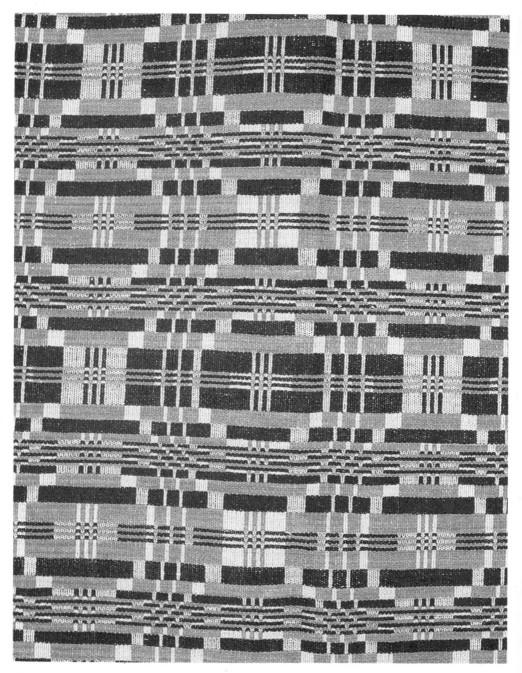

Woven Coverlet
L. 90 in   229 cm
W. 54 in   137 cm
Gift of Mr and Mrs James S.
Collins

This coverlet has been woven in two breadths, each 27 inches wide, and joined. The warp is natural coloured cotton and the weft tan and indigo blue wool

c 1840

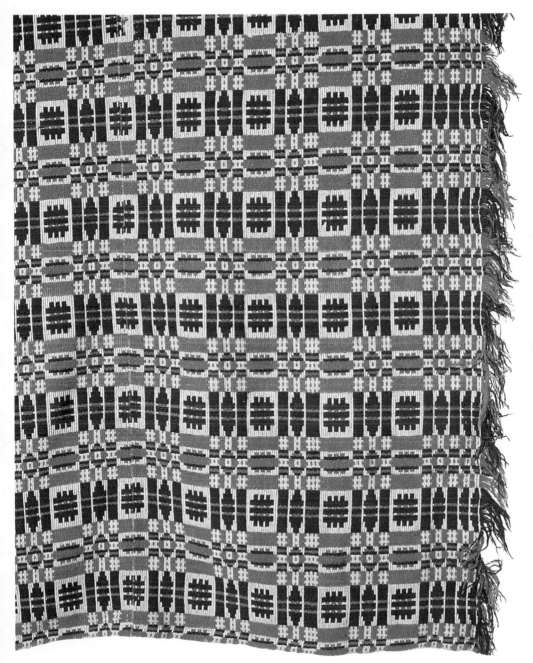

Woven Coverlet
L. 79 in   201 cm
W. 64 in   163 cm
Gift of Mrs Helen Mortensen

Double weave coverlet made in two pieces and joined. Both warp
and weft are of deep rose pink and indigo blue wool

Mid nineteenth century

Woven Coverlet
L. 100 in   254 cm
W. 80 in   203 cm

Jacquard weave coverlet with a warp of natural cotton and an indigo blue woollen weft. The border has a pattern of eagles, Independence Hall and Masonic emblems. In one corner is woven 'Agriculture and Manufactures are the foundation of our Independence July 4 1829' The name Mary Pulver has been woven on each side, presumably the name of the person for whom the coverlet was woven instead of the more usual weaver's name.

1829

Woven Coverlet
L. 96 in   244 cm
W. 36 in   91 cm
Gift of Mrs Mary Shaw

Woven on a Jacquard loom with natural cotton warp and weft of red and two shades of blue wool, this piece is just one half of a coverlet. It is fringed along one side and at the bottom.

The inscription reads 'Mary Leib 1840'. This part coverlet was found in the hope chest of Margaretta Boone Wintersteen of Port Carbon, Pennsylvania. As there were very few female jacquard weavers at this time the name Mary Leib would probably refer to the person for whom the coverlet was made.

Pennsylvania
1840

Woven Coverlet
L. 82 in   208 cm
W. 79 in   201 cm
Gift of Miss Nancy Hay

Jacquard weave coverlet with a natural cotton warp and red, green and indigo wool weft. There is a fringe on three sides. The inscription in the bottom border reads 'Latest Improved P Warrented M by H. Stager, Mount Joy'. Henry F. Stager (1820–1888) was weaving in Mount Joy, Lancaster Co., Pennsylvania by 1843.

c 1845

Woven Coverlet
L. 94 in   239 cm
W. 77 in   196 cm
Gift of Miss Mary Hoxie Jones

Jacquard weave coverlet with a warp of natural linen. The weft is natural linen with grey/green and mustard coloured wool. The formalised flower motifs are repeated in rectangles and a fringe has been added. The inscription reads 'Made by Thomas Marsteller Lo Saucon 1846'. Marsteller was born in Pennsylvania about 1812 and was weaving in Lower Saucon by 1842.

Pennsylvania
1842

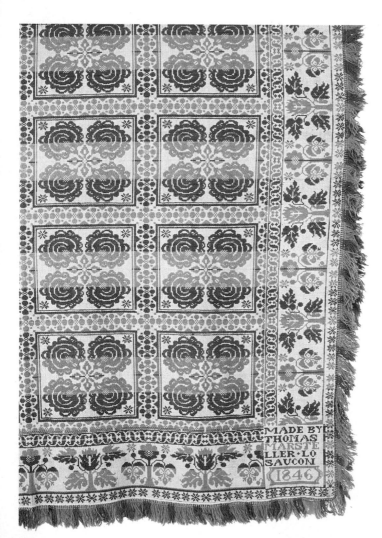

Woven Coverlet
L. 87 in   221 cm
W. 74 in   188 cm
*Gift of Colonel and Mrs Harold
Beverly Chase Jr.*

Jacquard coverlet woven in two pieces and joined. The warp is natural cotton and the weft red, green and blue wool. It is fringed on three sides. The inscription reads 'W. Jarvis, Chesterville, Ohio'

1850

Woven Coverlet
L. 84 in   213 cm
W. 75 in   191 cm
Gift of Mrs Adele Ingraham

Double weave Jacquard coverlet made with natural cotton warp and a hand spun, home dyed olive green wool weft. There is a fringe on three sides.

The patriotic design includes the bust of George Washington in the four corners and two horses, an eagle and two banners which read 'Hail 1869'

The inscription reads 'Made by Philip Schum, Lancaster, Pennsylvania' a professional weaver.

Philip Schum (1814–1880) was born in Germany and settled in Lancaster Co., Pennsylvania after 1844. He established a business which also produced carpets, blankets, yarns and flannels
1869

Knitted Coverlets

Fine knitting was well established in Egypt by the fifth century AD. The Arabs were expert knitters and so perhaps it was Arab traders who first taught knitting to the peoples of the Mediterranean, whence it spread to Europe and eventually to the American continent.

In mediaeval days most knitting was done by men, who had to serve a six-year apprenticeship. The invention in 1589 of a machine to knit stockings had little impact on knitting in the home, where knitting was a necessity, sometimes used as an alternative to weaving. Children were taught to knit at an early age. By the time the first colonists reached America domestic knitting was well established.

During the late eighteenth and early nineteenth centuries imported laces were very expensive and women began to make very fine knitted lace, which imitated the bobbin and needle-point laces, and used it to decorate both clothing and household linen. This form of knitting continued to be popular until the end of the century.

Bedcovers were made from individual squares, knitted in unbleached cotton yarn on very fine needles. Knitting started in one corner of the square with just one or three stitches. These were increased as knitting progressed until the diagonal was reached, when the number of stitches decreased, so forming a perfect square. The finished squares were joined together, as with patchwork blocks, often with crochet. After a knitted or crochet border had been added and bedcover was washed and bleached, so that it turned white and the stitches, having shrunk, were packed tightly together.

Knitted Coverlet
L. 114 in   290 cm
W. 90 in   229 cm

White cotton bedspread knitted in squares which have been joined together. The 5 inch border is also knitted.
Nineteenth century

Knitted Coverlet
L. 90 in   229 cm
W. 110 in   280 cm
Gift of Mr G. A. Brooker

The squares have been knitted in the pattern known as 'Mrs Cooledge's Grandmother's pattern'. The border is knitted. White cotton

Maryland
c 1850

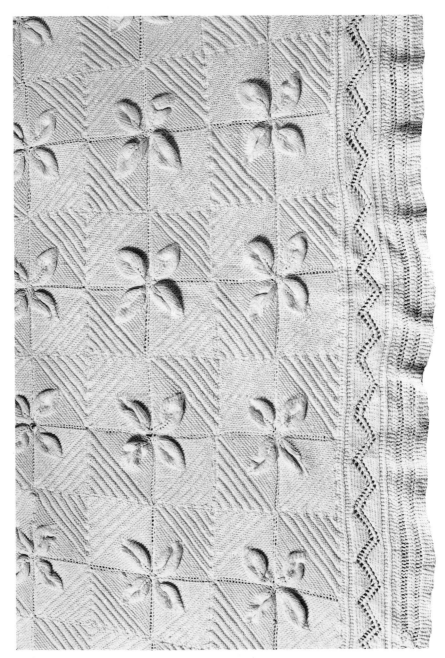

Bibliography

Binney, E. *Homage to Amanda*. R. K. Press, San Francisco, 1984

Bishop, R. and E. Safanda. *A Gallery of Amish Quilts*. Dutton, New York, 1976

Burnham, H. and Dorothy. *Keep Me Warm One Night – Woven Coverlets in Eastern Canada*. University of Toronto Press and Royal Ontario Museum, 1972

Carlisle, Lilian B. *Pieced Work and Applique Quilts at the Shelburne Museum*. Vermont, 1957

Clabburn, Pamela. *Patchwork*. Shire Books. 1983

Colby, Averil. *Patchwork*. Batsford, 1958

Colby, Averil. *Quilting*. Batsford, 1972

Davison, M and Christa Mayer-Thurman. *Coverlets*. The Art Institute of Chicago, 1973

Ferrero, Hedges and Silber. *Hearts and Hands*. The Influence of American Quilts on Women and Society. Quilt Digest Press, San Francisco, 1987

Finley, Ruth. *Old Patchwork Quilts*. Bell, 1929

Fitzrandolph, M. *Traditional Quilting*. Batsford, 1953

Fitzrandolph, M. and F. M. Fletcher. *Quilting*. Dryad Press

Graves, Sylvia. *History of Needlework Tools and Accessories*. David and Charles, 1973

Gutcheon, Beth. *The Perfect Patchwork Primer*. Penguin, 1973

Haders, Phyllis. *Sunshine and Shadow*. Main Street Press, New York, 1976

Hake, Elizabeth. *English Quilting*. Batsford, 1937

Hall, Eliza Calvert. *A Book of Handwoven Coverlets*. Little Brown & Co. 1914

Hall, Carrie and Rose Kretsinger. *The Romance of the Patchwork Quilt in America*. Bonanza Books, New York, 1935

Hammond, Joyce D. *Tifaifai and Quilts of Polynesia*. University of Hawaii Press, 1986

Heisey, John W. *A Checklist of American Coverlet Weavers*. Colonial Williamsburg Foundation, 1978

Holstein, Jonathan. *The Pieced Quilt – An American Design Tradition*. New York Graphic Society, Greenwich, Connecticut, 1975

Ickis, Marguerite. *The Standard Book of Quiltmaking*. Dover, 1949

Jones, Stella M. *Hawaiian Quilts*. Honolulu, 1973

Lasansky, Jeannette. *In The Heart of Pennsylvania – 19th and 20th Century Quiltmaking Traditions*. Lewisburg, Pennsylvania, 1985

Lasansky, Jeannette. *Pieced by Mother*. Lewisburg, Pennsylvania, 1987

Lipsett, Linda Otto. *Remember Me*. The Quilt Digest Press. San Francisco, 1985

Montgomery, Florence. *Printed Textiles*. English and American Cottons and Linens 1700–1850. Viking Press, New York, 1970

Montgomery, Florence. *Textiles in America, 1650–1870*. W. W. Norton & Co. New York and London, 1984

Orlofsky, Myron and Patsy. *Quilts in America*. McGraw Hill, 1975
Osler, Dorothy. *Traditional British Quilts*. Batsford, 1987
Rae, Janet. *The Quilts of the British Isles*. Constable, 1987
Safford, C. and Robert Bishop. *America's Quilts and Coverlets*. Dutton, New York, 1972
Seward, Linda. *The Complete Book of Patchwork, Quilting and Applique*. Mitchell Beazley, 1987
Walker, Michele. *Quiltmaking*. Ebury Press. London, 1985
Webster, Marie. *Quilts, Their Story and How to Make Them* Doubleday, New York, 1915
W. I. Books. *The Complete Book of Patchwork and Quilting*. Ed. Valerie Jackson, 1985
Woodard, Thomas and Blanche Greenstein. *Crib Quilts and Other Small Wonders*. Dutton, New York, 1981
Betterton, Shiela. *Quilts and Coverlets from the American Museum*, 1978 and 1982
American Quilt Study Group. *Uncoverings*, Vols. 1–8, San Francisco
The Quilt Digest Nos. 1–6. Quilt Digest Press, San Francisco
The Quilters' Guild. The Quilter (published quarterly)

Index

The author
When Shiela Betterton came to the Museum as a Guide, in 1963, she noticed that the quilting patterns on some of the American quilts were similar to those on quilts made in her native Northumberland. This was the beginning of her extensive research into patchwork and quilting as practiced all over the world. The quilt collection at the museum grew rapidly and in 1974 she was appointed the first Textile and Needlework Specialist. She has lectured on patchwork and quilting all over the British Isles and also in the United States of America.

Publications include

    for the American Museum
    American Textiles and Needlework
    The American Quilt Tradition
    Quilts and Coverlets from the American Museum
    Rugs from the American Museum

Other books include

    The Complete Book of Needlework, co-author, ed. Mary Gostelow
    The Royal School of Needlework Book of Needlework and
        Embroidery, co-author, ed. Lanto Synge.

She has also written articles for magazines and quilting journals.

THE AMERICAN MUSEUM IN BRITAIN, the only comprehensive museum of Americana in Europe, is located at Claverton Manor, a country house near the city of Bath. The house, situated above the valley of the river Avon, was designed in 1820 by Sir Jeffry Wyatville, architect to King George IV.

The museum tells the story of American life from about 1680 until 1860 through a series of completely furnished rooms, some of which have original panelling brought from the United States. Contrasts in the life of colonial New England are shown in the Puritan Keeping Room of the 1680's and the cosy tavern kitchen of the 1770's with its beehive oven and well-protected bar, in the blue-green panelled living room from Lee, New Hampshire, and the mid-eighteenth-century parlour of Captain Perley, who led his Minute Men at the battle of Bunker Hill. The sophistication of the parlours from Colchester, Connecticut and Baltimore, Maryland, introduces the period of the New Republic. An early nineteenth-century country style bedroom contrasts with the elegance of the Greek Revival dining room of New York and the richly ornate bedroom from New Orleans at the time of the Civil War.

In addition there are galleries devoted to the American Indian, and Pennsylvania Dutch, the religious community of the Shakers, and the isolated Spanish colonists of New Mexico. There are further exhibits on the Opening of the West, Whaling (with a Captain's cabin reproduced from the last of the great Yankee whalers), Textiles (with a fine collection of quilts and hooked rugs), Pewter, Glass and Silver.

The Park and formal gardens provide an ideal setting for outdoor exhibits including a Conestoga wagon and an Indian Tepee. The old stables, adapted to make a gallery, house the Folk Art collection; nearby is a replica of George Washington's rose and flower garden at Mount Vernon, Virginia, and on the terrace is a herb garden and herb shop. There is also an American Arboretum, Fernery and Apple Orchard.

Open 2 to 5 every day (except Monday) from the end of March to the end of October. Out of normal opening hours, private tours can be arranged on application to the Secretary.

Further information may be obtained from The Secretary, The American Museum in Britain, Claverton Manor, Bath, BA2 7BD. Telephone Bath (0225) 60503.